Uniqueness
In me
Creates Posititvity

Copyright © 2024 Andrea Hubert Villatoro

All rights reserved. This book or any portion thereof may not be reproduced or used in any manner whatsoever without the publisher's express written permission except for the use of brief quotations in a book review or scholarly journal.
ISBN: 9798333128782

Designed and produced by Calm Expressions Publishing at www.ebonystubbs.com

Dedication & Inspiration:

Ephesians 1: 16-19 (ESV)

Thank you, Lord, for your spirit and guidance with this assignment.

To My Deceased Mother, Shirley Edward Vaughns.
To My Deceased Brother, Lonnie Earl Hubert Jr.
My children Noah Antonio Villatoro, Lydia Shirrelle Villatoro, Nelson Emmanuel Villatoro, and future grandchildren (Legacy).

Dear Unique Parent

Thank you for allowing this partnership as you affirm the uniqueness of your early reader. Uniqueness in me is designed to motivate readers to stay active and engage in positive activities.

Uniqueness in me enhances the teaching of primary colors, days of the week, sight words, and improving vocabulary.

This contribution to literature demonstrates how to:

1. Encourage your child to read daily.

2. We ask that you add "Uniqueness in me Creates Positivity" to their morning routine.

3. Instruct your child to be active daily with the daily activities in this book.

4. Enjoy finding things that match the color of the day. Remember to:

• Send clips of your unique child/student enjoying a unique activity.

• Share to our social media! IG@IamUnique7DaysAweek and use #UniqueActivity

Dear Unique Educator

This contribution to literature enhances:
1. Phonemic Awareness.

2. Encourages early reading to promote confident readers.

3. Promotes interactive learning with literacy

Dear Unique Friend

Hello friend! My name is Unique; I learned how to read when I was five during Grahm Time. I chose a book to read with my grandmother, and we created games based on what we had read. I do the day's activity and write about it in my journal. You can, too!
Send a video to me: solutionminded99@gmail.com

You can Paint

I will paint a picture that is nice for me
I will show my parents and let them see
With talent and creativity
I paint and feel free to just be me
The more I paint the more I explore
My painting evolves more and more
All it takes is concentration
I think with my imagination.

Listen to Music

Music takes me to my happy place
Music will put a smile on my face
Music will make me sing along
With music I will listen to my favorite songs
I will listen to my music When I play
I will listen to my music outside today.

You can Laugh

I love to laugh with my family
Come to our picnic and you will see
How we bond connect and laugh a lot
And the good food really hits the spot
Someone says a joke and we burst into laughter
My family's motto is to live happily ever after.

You can Sing

Singing will make you smile
Singing will bring you joy
It does not matter
If you're a girl or a boy
Kids karaoke sing a song or two
You will enjoy yourself when you are through
Sing and clap Sing and dance
Whatever you do just give it a chance.

You can Dance

1,2,3,4,5,6,7,8
Come on, let's dance and do
not be late
You can do some movement
and count the beat
Just lift your hands
and move your feet
Turn up your music
and get out of bed
You have to move your body
and shake a leg.

You can Play

Yes, it is time to go and play
I am all worn out by the end of
the day
My friends are with me in my yard
Sports all day gets you rewards

It is hard to keep up and not get
tired
But having fun is how I am wired
I love my friends, and they love
me
We always act like family.

You can Journal

I write in my journal all the time,
I write out my ideas that cross my mind
I write out my affirmations
To remind me I can win
At anything I put my mind to
From beginning to the end
I write out the good things from my day
It helps me feel confident about anything I say.

Made in the USA
Columbia, SC
16 August 2024